First Nature Books

The Grasshopper

Gunilla Ingves

Adam & Charles Black · London

The First Nature Books series

1 The Fly
2 The Ladybird
3 The Grasshopper
4 The Snail
5 The Mushroom
6 The Dandelion

Published by A & C Black (Publishers) Limited
35 Bedford Row, London WC1R 4JH
First published by Natur och Kultur, Sweden
under the series title *Har du sett på...*
© Gunilla Ingves text and pictures 1978
© 1983 English text A & C Black (Publishers)
Limited

This edition arranged with the help of Angus
Hudson, London
Filmset by Euroset Typesetting Limited,
London
Printed and Bound in Great Britain
by Purnell and Sons (Book Production) Ltd.,
Paulton, Bristol

It is a hot, sunny day in August. A female grasshopper is sitting still in the green grass.

3

She can hear the sound of other insects up in the trees above her.

Suddenly she hears the noise of a male grasshopper. He is brown. The female grasshopper jumps towards the sound.

5

Another male grasshopper turns up. But the first one chases him off with an angry noise. He wants the female all for himself.

The male grasshopper goes on making his noise. The female answers him but she can't make as much noise. The two grasshoppers mate.

7

After a few days, the
female grasshopper lays
eggs on the ground. She
covers the eggs with a
sticky liquid. The liquid
goes hard and protects
the eggs.

Soon after, the male and female grasshopper both die.

Next spring, young grasshoppers hatch from the eggs. The tiny young look like their parents but they don't have any wings.

The young grasshoppers
jump all over the place on
their long legs. They even
jump on to a dandelion!
They start to nibble the
fresh green grass.

The young grasshoppers
grow and grow until their skins burst.
This doesn't matter because there is a
new skin underneath. They have tiny
wings now, too. Young grasshoppers
change their skins several times before
they are grown-up. This is called
moulting.

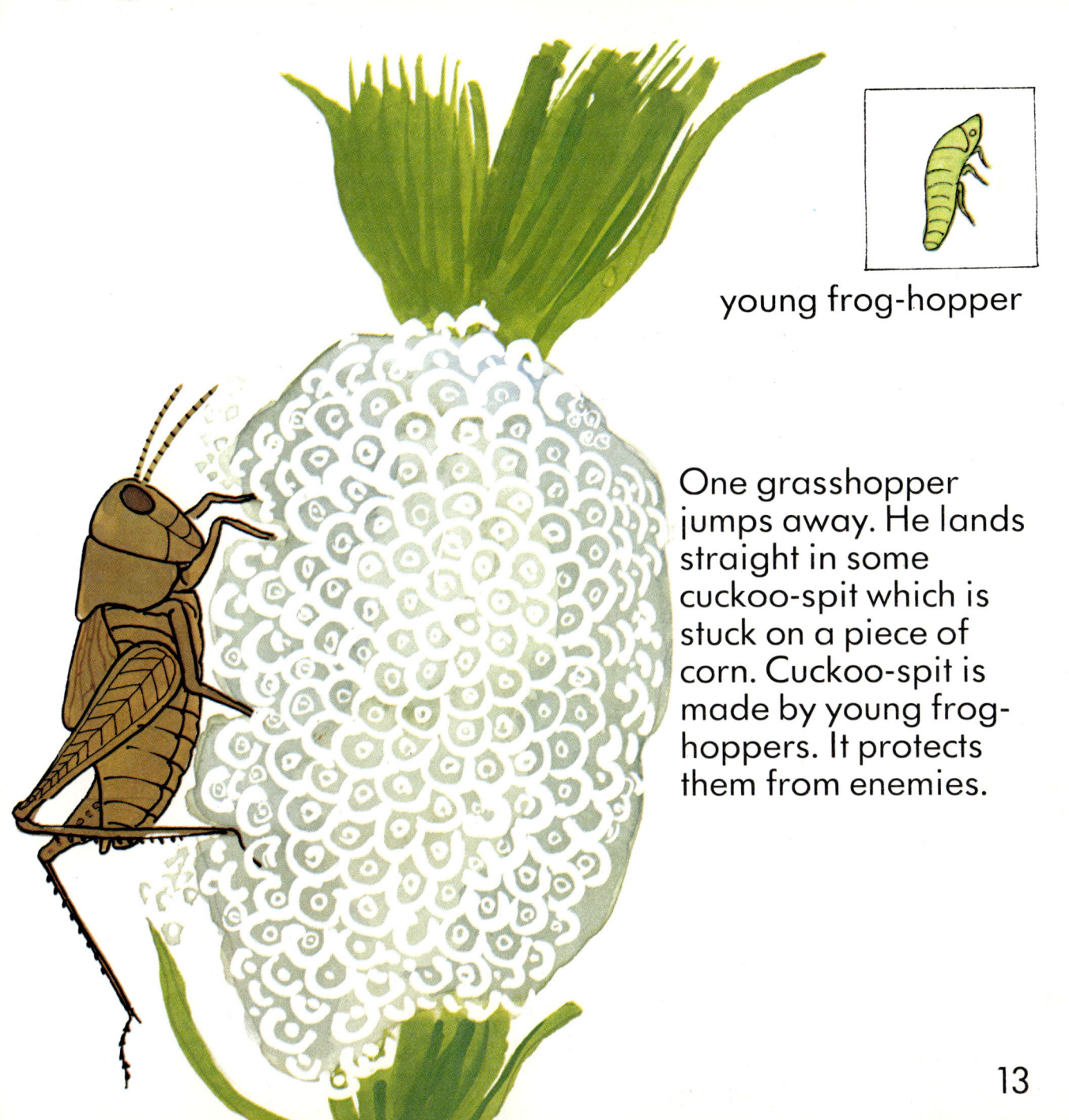

young frog-hopper

One grasshopper jumps away. He lands straight in some cuckoo-spit which is stuck on a piece of corn. Cuckoo-spit is made by young frog-hoppers. It protects them from enemies.

But grasshoppers and frog-hoppers aren't enemies. So the young grasshopper jumps down and wipes the spit off his legs. Then he washes his face and dries himself on the grass.

Off he jumps again. This time he lands straight in a spider's web. He struggles and kicks to get away. But he can't because the web is sticky.

15

Out comes a huge, fat
spider. It will eat the
grasshopper if it can.
The spider walks
slowly towards the
grasshopper.

Then a girl runs through the grass and knocks the web. The spider is frightened and turns round. The girls sees the grasshopper and picks him out of the web. She looks at him carefully.

17

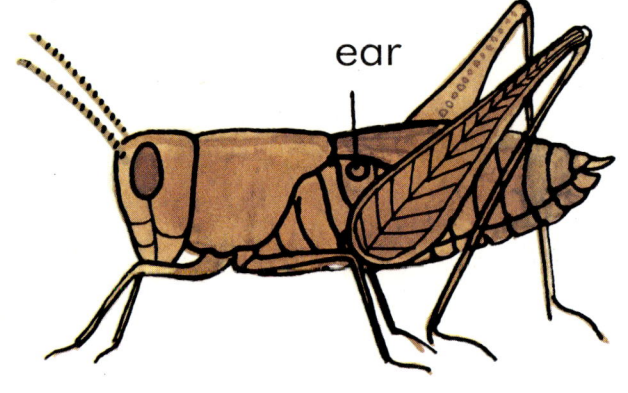

ear

The grasshopper has two eyes and two short feelers called antennae. He uses the antennae to smell. He has two strong jaws on his mouth called mandibles. They help him to chew grass and leaves. His ears are really only two small holes in the middle of his back.

Grasshoppers have two wings. At the moment, they are very short. When the grasshopper is grown-up, his wings will be as long as his whole body.

The grasshopper has four short legs at the front and two very long legs at the back. The insides of his back legs are knobbly. When the male grasshopper calls to the female, he rubs the knobs on his thighs against the hard edges of his wings.

The girl lets the grasshopper go. He jumps off and joins some other young grasshoppers. They sit in the sun. Suddenly . . .

19

. . . a big tabby cat comes along. It lifts a paw to catch one of the grasshoppers but they all jump away.

One grasshopper jumps straight into the open mouth of a frog. And that's the end of him!

It is July. The grasshoppers moult for the very last time. They are now fully grown. This means the males can make their special noise. They rub their wings and thighs together.

Then it starts to rain.
Grasshoppers hate it
when it's cold and wet.
They jump for cover
under a large
mushroom.

Next day the sun shines again. The grasshoppers hurry out into the warm sunshine. The males start to make their noise. You can hear them all day long and far into the night, too.